AND THEN THERE WERE NONE

Agatha Christie

TECHNICAL DIRECTOR Maxwell Krohn
EDITORIAL DIRECTOR Justin Kestler
MANAGING EDITOR Ben Florman

SERIES EDITORS Boomie Aglietti, Justin Kestler
PRODUCTION Christian Lorentzen, Camille Murphy

WRITERS Benjamin Lytal, Ross Douthat
EDITORS Dennis Quinio, Boomie Aglietti

This edition published by Spark Publishing

Spark Publishing
A Division of SparkNotes LLC
120 Fifth Avenue, 8th Floor
New York, NY 10011

02 03 04 05 SN 9 8 7 6 5 4 3 2 1

Please send all comments and questions or report errors to
feedback@sparknotes.com.

Library of Congress information available upon request

Printed and bound in the United States

RRD-C

ISBN 1-58663-468-2

INTRODUCTION: STOPPING TO BUY SPARKNOTES ON A SNOWY EVENING

Whose words these are you *think* you know.
Your paper's due tomorrow, though;
We're glad to see you stopping here
To get some help before you go.

Lost your course? You'll find it here.
Face tests and essays without fear.
Between the words, good grades at stake:
Get great results throughout the year.

Once school bells caused your heart to quake
As teachers circled each mistake.
Use SparkNotes and no longer weep,
Ace every single test you take.

Yes, books are lovely, dark, and deep,
But only what you grasp you keep,
With hours to go before you sleep,
With hours to go before you sleep.

CONTENTS

NOTE: This SparkNote refers to the St. Martin's Press edition of *And Then There Were None*. The novel was originally published under the title *Ten Little Indians*.

CONTEXT

AGATHA CHRISTIE WAS BORN Agatha Mary Clarissa Miller on September 5, 1890, in Torquay, England. In 1914 she married Colonel Archibald Christie, an aviator in the Royal Flying Corps. They had a daughter, Rosalind, and divorced in 1928. By that time, Christie had begun writing mystery stories, initially in response to a dare from her sister. Her first novel, *The Mysterious Affair at Styles,* was published in 1920 and featured the debut of one of her most famous characters, the Belgian sleuth Hercule Poirot. Christie would go on to become the world's best-selling writer of mystery novels.

By the time Christie began writing, the mystery novel was a well-established genre with definite rules. Edgar Allan Poe pioneered the mystery genre in his short story "Murders in the Rue Morgue," and writers like Sir Arthur Conan Doyle carried on the tradition Poe began. In traditional mysteries like Poe's and Doyle's, the story is told from the perspective of a detective-protagonist (or a friend of the detective, like Sherlock Holmes's companion, Dr. Watson) as he or she examines clues and pursues a killer. At the end of the novel, the detective unmasks the murderer and sums up the case, explaining the crime and clearing up mysterious events. As the story unfolds, the reader gets access to exactly the same information as the detective, which makes the mystery novel a kind of game in which the reader has a chance to solve the case for him- or herself.

Fairly early in her career, in 1926, Christie came under fire for writing an "unfair" mystery novel. In *The Murder of Roger Ackroyd,* the killer turns out to be the narrator, and many readers and critics felt that this was too deceptive a plot twist. Christie was unapologetic, however, and today *The Murder of Roger Ackroyd* is considered a masterpiece of the detective genre.

And Then There Were None, written in 1939, breaks more rules of the mystery genre. No detective solves the case, the murderer escapes from the law's grasp, and the plot construction makes guessing the killer's identity nearly impossible. Despite this rule-breaking, or perhaps because of it, *And Then There Were None* ranks as one of Christie's most popular and critically acclaimed novels. It was made into a stage play, and several film versions have been produced, the most celebrated of which is the 1945 version starring Barry Fitzgerald and Walter Huston.

In all, Christie produced eighty novels and short-story collections, most of them featuring either Poirot or her other famous sleuth, the elderly spinster Miss Marple. She also wrote four works of nonfiction and fourteen plays, including *The Mousetrap*, the longest-running play in history. Eventually, Christie married an archaeologist named Sir Max Mallowan, whose trips to the Middle East provided the setting for a number of her novels. In 1971, Queen Elizabeth II awarded Christie the title of Dame Commander of the British Empire. Christie died in Oxfordshire, England, on January 12, 1976.

PLOT OVERVIEW

IGHT PEOPLE, ALL STRANGERS to each other, are invited to Indian Island, off the English coast. Vera Claythorne, a former governess, thinks she has been hired as a secretary; Philip Lombard, an adventurer, and William Blore, an ex-detective, think they have been hired to look out for trouble over the weekend; Dr. Armstrong thinks he has been hired to look after the wife of the island's owner. Emily Brent, General Macarthur, Tony Marston, and Judge Wargrave think they are going to visit old friends.

When they arrive on the island, the guests are greeted by Mr. and Mrs. Rogers, the butler and housekeeper, who report that the host, someone they call Mr. Owen, will not arrive until the next day. That evening, as all the guests gather in the drawing room after an excellent dinner, they hear a recorded voice accusing each of them of a specific murder committed in the past and never uncovered. They compare notes and realize that none of them, including the servants, knows "Mr. Owen," which suggests that they were brought here according to someone's strange plan.

As they discuss what to do, Tony Marston chokes on poisoned whiskey and dies. Frightened, the party retreats to bed, where almost everyone is plagued by guilt and memories of their crimes. Vera Claythorne notices the similarity between the death of Marston and the first verse of a nursery rhyme, "Ten Little Indians," that hangs in each bedroom.

The next morning the guests find that Mrs. Rogers apparently died in her sleep. The guests hope to leave that morning, but the boat that regularly delivers supplies to the island does not show up. Blore, Lombard, and Armstrong decide that the deaths must have been murders and determine to scour the island in search of the mysterious Mr. Owen. They find no one, however. Meanwhile, the oldest guest, General Macarthur, feels sure he is going to die and goes to look out at the ocean. Before lunch, Dr. Armstrong finds the general dead of a blow to the head.

The remaining guests meet to discuss their situation. They decide that one of them must be the killer. Many make vague accusations, but Judge Wargrave reminds them that the existing evidence suggests any of them could be the killer. Afternoon and dinner pass restlessly, and everyone goes to bed, locking his or her door before doing so. The next morning, they find that Rogers has been killed while chopping wood in preparation for breakfast. At this point, the guests feel sure the murders are being carried out according to the dictates of the nursery rhyme. Also, they realize that the dining-room table initially featured ten Indian figures, but with each death one of the figures disappears.

After breakfast, Emily Brent feels slightly giddy, and she remains alone at the table for a while. She is soon found dead, her neck having been injected with poison. At this point, Wargrave initiates an organized search of everyone's belongings, and anything that could be used as a weapon is locked away. The remaining guests sit together, passing time and casting suspicious looks at each other. Finally, Vera goes to take a bath, but she is startled by a piece of seaweed hanging from her ceiling and cries out. Blore, Lombard, and Armstrong run to help her, only to return downstairs to find Wargrave draped in a curtain that resembles courtroom robes and bearing a red mark on his forehead. Armstrong examines the body and reports that Wargrave has been shot in the head.

That night, Blore hears footsteps in the hall; upon checking, he finds that Armstrong is not in his room. Blore and Lombard search for Armstrong, but they cannot find him anywhere in the house or on the island. When they return from searching, they discover another Indian figure missing from the table.

Vera, Lombard, and Blore go outside, resolving to stay in the safety of the open land. Blore decides to go back into the house to get food. The other two hear a crash, and they find someone has pushed a statue out of a second-story window, killing Blore as he approached the house. Vera and Lombard retreat to the shore, where they find Armstrong's drowned body on the beach. Convinced that Lombard is the killer, Vera steals Lombard's gun and shoots him. She returns to her bedroom to rest, happy to have survived. But upon finding a noose waiting for her in her room, she feels a strange compulsion to enact the last line of the nursery rhyme, and hangs herself.

The mystery baffles the police until a manuscript in a bottle is found. The late Judge Wargrave wrote the manuscript explaining that he planned the murders because he wanted to punish those whose crimes are not punishable under law. Wargrave frankly admits to his own lust for blood and pleasure in seeing the guilty punished. When a doctor told Wargrave he was dying, he decided to die in a blaze, instead of letting his life trickle away. He discusses how he chose his victims and how he did away with Marston, Mr. and Mrs. Rogers, Macarthur, and Emily Brent. Wargrave then describes how he tricked Dr. Armstrong into helping him fake his own death, promising to meet the doctor by the cliffs to discuss a plan. When Armstrong arrived, Wargrave pushed him over the edge into the sea, then returned to the house and pretended to be dead. His ruse enabled him to dispose of the rest of the guests without drawing their suspicion. Once Vera hanged herself on a noose that he prepared for her, Wargrave planned to shoot himself in such a way that his body would fall onto the bed as if it had been laid there. Thus, he hoped, the police would find ten dead bodies on an empty island.

CHARACTER LIST

Judge Lawrence Wargrave A recently retired judge. Wargrave is a highly intelligent old man with a commanding personality. As the characters begin to realize that a murderer is hunting them, Wargrave's experience and air of authority make him a natural leader for the group. He lays out evidence, organizes searches, and ensures that weapons are locked away safely. Wargrave's guilt is revealed at the end of the novel in a confession that illuminates the characteristics that drive him to commit the series of murders: a strong sense of justice combined with a sadistic delight in murdering.

Vera Claythorne A former governess who comes to Indian Island purportedly to serve as a secretary to Mrs. Owen. Vera wants to escape a past in which she killed a small boy in her care, Cyril Hamilton, so that the man she loved would inherit Cyril's estate. Although the coroner cleared her of blame, Vera's lover abandoned her. Vera is one of the most intelligent and capable characters in the novel, but she also suffers from attacks of hysteria, feels guilty about her crime, and reacts nervously to the uncanny events on the island. The "Ten Little Indians" poem has a powerful effect on her.

Philip Lombard A mysterious, confident, and resourceful man who seems to have been a mercenary soldier in Africa. Lombard is far bolder and more cunning than most of the other characters, traits that allow him to survive almost until the end of the novel. His weakness is his chivalrous attitude toward women, particularly Vera, with whom he has a number of private conversations. He cannot think of her as a potential killer, and he underestimates her resourcefulness, which proves a fatal mistake.

Dr. Edward James Armstrong A gullible, slightly timid doctor. Armstrong often draws the suspicion of the other guests because of his medical knowledge. He is a recovering alcoholic who once accidentally killed a patient by operating on her while drunk. Armstrong, while professionally successful, has a weak personality, making him the perfect tool for the murderer. He has spent his whole life pursuing respectability and public success, and is unable to see beneath people's exteriors.

William Henry Blore A former police inspector. Blore is a well-built man whose experience often inspires others to look to him for advice. As a policeman, he was corrupt and framed a man named Landor at the behest of a criminal gang. On the island, he acts boldly and frequently takes initiative, but he also makes frequent blunders. He constantly suspects the wrong person, and his boldness often verges on foolhardiness.

Emily Brent An old, ruthlessly religious woman who reads her Bible every day. The recording accuses Emily Brent of killing Beatrice Taylor, a servant whom she fired upon learning that Beatrice was pregnant out of wedlock. Beatrice subsequently killed herself. Unlike the other characters, Emily Brent feels convinced of her own righteousness and does not express the slightest remorse for her actions.

Thomas Rogers The dignified butler. Rogers continues to be a proper servant even after his wife is found dead and the bodies begin piling up. The recording accuses Rogers and his wife of letting their former employer die because they stood to inherit money from her.

General John Gordon Macarthur The oldest guest. Macarthur is accused of sending a lieutenant, Arthur Richmond, to his death during World War I because Richmond was his wife's lover. Once the first murders take place, Macarthur, already guilt-ridden about his crime, becomes resigned to his death and sits by the sea waiting for it to come to him.

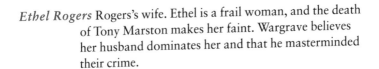

Ethel Rogers Rogers's wife. Ethel is a frail woman, and the death of Tony Marston makes her faint. Wargrave believes her husband dominates her and that he masterminded their crime.

Anthony Marston A rich, athletic, handsome youth. Tony Marston likes to drive recklessly and seems to lack a conscience. He killed two small children in a car accident caused by his speeding, but shows no remorse.

Isaac Morris A shady, criminal character hired by the murderer to make the arrangements for the island. Morris allegedly peddled drugs to a young woman and drove her to suicide.

CHARACTER LIST

ANALYSIS OF MAJOR CHARACTERS

JUDGE WARGRAVE

A recently retired judge, Wargrave is intelligent, cold, and commanding. During his years on the bench, he had a reputation as a "hanging judge"—a judge who persuaded juries to bring back guilty verdicts and sentenced many convicted criminals to death. Christie describes Wargrave as wizened and ugly, with a "frog-like face[,] ... tortoise-like neck," and "pale shrewd little eyes"; his ugliness makes his appearance more forbidding. Once the situation on Indian Island becomes clear and the guests realize that a murderer is hunting them, they look to Wargrave for leadership, and he obliges. He is the first to insist publicly that they are dealing with a homicidal maniac, and the first to acknowledge that the killer must be part of their group. When leading group meetings on the island, he often acts like a judge presiding over a court. Wargrave analyzes evidence, authorizes searches both of the island and of people's possessions, and takes charge of drugs and other potential weapons, ensuring that they are safely locked away.

It is partially Wargrave's experience with criminal proceedings that makes the others go along with his leadership, but he also has a confidence-inspiring ability to project an air of cold reason in a time of crisis. In a standard detective story, Wargrave's behavior would make him the detective figure, using his experience with the criminal mind to unmask the killer. But as we learn at the close of the novel, when a local fisherman recovers his confession, Wargrave himself is the killer. He plans the entire enterprise, selects his ten victims, buys the island, and then pretends to be one of the group. Despite his identity as murderer, however, Wargrave is not entirely unlike the detective in a traditional mystery story. Since all of his victims are supposedly guilty of murder, Wargrave, like the detective, acts as an agent of justice, making sure that murderers are punished for their crimes. Nevertheless, in spite of his victims' obvious guilt and Wargrave's insistence that he would not let an innocent person suffer, we are unlikely to find him a sympathetic character. Far from being a disinterested agent of justice, Wargrave is a sadist, taking perverse pleasure in murder. As a boy, he killed insects for sport, and he brings the same zeal to his task on Indian Island. He never shows pity for his victims; instead, he regards them as pawns to move around and kill in order to create what he terms a "work of art"— his perfect killing spree.

VERA CLAYTHORNE

Vera Claythorne is a former governess who is working as a "games mistress at a third-class school" when the novel begins. She takes a summer job on Indian Island, believing that she has been hired to serve as a secretary to a Mrs. Una Owen. Like the other characters, Vera has a dark secret. At her last job, she was governess to a spoiled little rich boy named Cyril Hamilton. She let Cyril drown so that his relative, Hugo, would inherit his money and then be rich enough to marry her. An inquest cleared her of any wrongdoing, but Hugo, certain that Vera had let Cyril die, would have nothing more to do with her. Throughout the novel, Vera's guilty memories of her crime plague her. She often thinks of Hugo and feels as if he is watching her.

In some ways, Vera is one of the most intelligent and capable characters in the novel, which explains why she is one of the last people left standing. She outwits the resourceful Philip Lombard, who thinks she is a murderer, by stealing his gun and then summoning up the courage to shoot him when he leaps at her. Despite her strength, however, Vera is not emotionally stable. In addition to her recurrent bouts of guilt over Cyril's death, she is strongly affected by the almost supernatural nature of the events on the island and prone to attacks of nervous hysteria. More than anyone else, she fixates on the "Ten Little Indians" poem that lends an air of eerie inevitability to the murders. The confluence of these factors—her guilt, her tendency toward hysteria, and her fascination with the nursery rhyme—enables Wargrave to create a suggestive environment complete with a noose and the smell of the sea, which inspires Vera to hang herself and fulfill the last line of the poem.

PHILIP LOMBARD

Philip Lombard has the most mysterious past of anyone on the island. He is a world traveler and a former military man who seems to have served as a soldier of fortune in Africa. In the epilogue, one of the policemen describes him as having "been mixed up in some very curious shows abroad . . . [the] sort of fellow who might do several murders in some quiet out-of-the-way spot." He comes to Indian Island after Isaac Morris hires him, supposedly because Mr. Owen needs a "good man in a tight spot." Clearly a dangerous man, Lombard carries a gun and is frequently described as moving "like a panther." He is bold enough to initiate several searches of the island, perceptive enough to suspect Judge Wargrave of being the killer, and brave enough to voice his suspicions. Lombard is also honest: he owns up to his past misdeeds. When the recorded voice accuses him of leaving twenty-one men from an East African tribe to die in the bush, Lombard cheerfully admits to it, saying there was only enough food for himself and a friend, and so they took off with it. The other characters cannot bring themselves to admit their own guilt, but Lombard has no such qualms.

Lombard does display a weakness, however, that ultimately brings about his downfall: his chivalrous and old-fashioned attitude toward women. In the first group conversation about the murders, he suggests excluding the women from the list of potential suspects, since he considers them incapable of homicidal behavior. Lombard's tendency to underestimate women enables Vera to steal his gun and shoot him when he jumps at her. In a strange way, his death unites Vera and Lombard—they are the only characters to die at the hand of someone other than Wargrave.

THEMES, MOTIFS & SYMBOLS

THEMES

Themes are the fundamental and often universal ideas explored in a literary work.

THE ADMINISTRATION OF JUSTICE

Most murder mysteries examine justice—its violation, through the act of murder, and its restoration, through the work of a detective who solves the crime and ensures that the murderer pays for his or her deed. *And Then There Were None* examines justice, but it bends the formula by making the victims of murder people who committed murder themselves. Thus, the killings on Indian Island are arguably acts of justice. Judge Wargrave does the work of detective and murderer by picking out those who are guilty and punishing them.

Whether we accept the justice of the events on Indian Island depends on both whether we accept Wargrave's belief that all the murder victims deserve their deaths and whether we accept that Wargrave has the moral authority to pronounce and carry out the sentences. At least some of the murders are unjust if we do not consider all of Wargrave's victims murderers. Emily Brent, for example, did not actually kill her servant, Beatrice Taylor. Thus, one could argue that she deserves a lesser punishment for her sin.

Christie explores the line that divides those who act unjustly from those who seek to restore justice. She suggests that unjust behavior does not necessarily make someone bad and enforcing justice does not necessarily make someone good . Wargrave's victims, although they have violated the rules of moral behavior in the past, are, for the most part, far more likable and decent human beings than Wargrave. Although Wargrave serves justice in a technical sense, he is a cruel and unsympathetic man, and likely insane.

THE EFFECTS OF GUILT ON ONE'S CONSCIENCE

By creating a story in which every character has committed a crime, Christie explores different human responses to the burden of a guilty conscience. Beginning with the first moments after the recorded voice reveals the guests' crimes, each character takes a different approach to dealing with his or her guilt.

The characters who publicly and self-righteously deny their crimes are tormented by guilt in private. General Macarthur, for instance, brusquely dismisses the claim that he killed his wife's lover. By the following day, however, guilt so overwhelms him that he resignedly waits to die. Dr. Armstrong is equally dismissive of the charges against him, but he soon starts dreaming about the woman who died on his operating table.

On the other hand, the people who own up to their crimes are less likely to feel pangs of guilt. Lombard willingly admits to leaving tribesmen to die in the African bush, insisting that he did it to save his own life and would willingly do it again. Tony Marston readily owns up to running down the two children, and he displays no sense of having done anything wrong. Neither of the two men gives a moment's private thought to his crime.

While the ones who do not own up to their crimes feel the guiltiest, no such correlation exists between levels of guilt and likelihood of survival. Conscience has no bearing on who lives the longest, as is illustrated by the contrast between the last two characters left alive, Lombard and Vera. Lombard feels no guilt, and the air of doom that enshrouds the island doesn't affect him. Vera, on the other hand, is so guilt-ridden that she ends her life by succumbing to the seemingly inevitable conclusion of the "Ten Little Indians" poem and the aura of almost supernatural vengeance that pervades the novel.

The Danger of Reliance on Class Distinctions

And Then There Were None takes place in 1930s Britain, a society stratified into strict social classes. These distinctions play a subtle but important role in the novel. As the situation on the island becomes more and more desperate, social hierarchies continue to dictate behavior, and their persistence ultimately makes it harder for some characters to survive. Rogers continues to perform his butler's duties even after it becomes clear that a murderer is on the loose, and even after the murderer has killed his wife. Because it is expected of a man of his social class, Rogers washes up after people, remains downstairs to clean up after the others have gone to bed, and rises early in the morning to chop firewood. The separation from the group that his work necessitates makes it easy for the murderer to kill him. Additionally, the class-bound mentality of Dr. Armstrong

THEMES

proves disastrous for himself and others, as he refuses to believe that a respectable professional man like Wargrave could be the killer.

Motifs

Motifs are recurring structures, contrasts, or literary devices that can help to develop and inform the text's major themes.

The "Ten Little Indians" Poem
The "Ten Little Indians" rhyme guides the progression of the novel. The singsong, childish verses tell the story of the deaths of ten Indian boys and end with the line that gives the novel its title: "and then there were none." A framed copy of the rhyme hangs in every bedroom, and ten small Indian figures sit on the dining-room table. The murders are carried out to match, as closely as possible, the lines in the poem, and after each murder, one of the figures vanishes from the dining room. The overall effect is one of almost supernatural inevitability; eventually, all the characters realize that the next murder will match the next verse, yet they are unable to escape their fates. The poem affects Vera Claythorne more powerfully than it affects anyone else. She becomes obsessed with it, and when she eventually kills herself she is operating under the suggestive power of the poem's final verse.

Dreams and Hallucinations
Dreams and hallucinations recur throughout the novel, usually as a reflection of various characters' guilty consciences. Dr. Armstrong has a dream in which he operates on a person whose face is first Emily Brent's and then Tony Marston's. This dream likely grows out of Armstrong's memories of accidentally killing a woman on the operating table. Emily Brent seems to go into a trance while writing in her diary; she wakes from it to find the words "The murderer's name is Beatrice Taylor" scrawled across the page. Beatrice Taylor is the name of Emily Brent's former maid, who got pregnant and killed herself after Emily Brent fired her. Brent's unconscious scrawl demonstrates, if not her guilty conscience, at least her preoccupation with the death of her servant. Vera Claythorne often feels that Hugo Hamilton—her former lover, for whose sake she let a little boy drown—watches her, and whenever she smells the sea, she remembers the day the boy died, as if hallucinating.

SYMBOLS

Symbols are objects, characters, figures, or colors used to represent abstract ideas or concepts.

THE STORM

For most of the novel, a fierce storm cuts the island off from the outside world. This storm works as a plot device, for it both prevents anyone from escaping the island and allows the murderer free rein. At the same time, the violence of the weather symbolizes the violent acts taking place on Indian Island. The storm first breaks when the men carry the corpse of General Macarthur into the dining room, symbolizing the guests' dawning realization that a murderer is loose on the island.

THE MARK ON JUDGE WARGRAVE'S FOREHEAD

When Wargrave fakes his own death and then kills himself at the end of the novel, he leaves a red gunshot wound on his forehead— first a fake wound, then a real wound. This wound, as he points out in his confession, mirrors the brand that God placed upon the forehead of Cain, the first murderer in the Bible. It symbolizes Wargrave's self-admitted links to Cain: both are evil men and murderers.

FOOD

When the characters arrive on the island, they are treated to an excellent dinner. Soon, however, they are reduced to eating cold tongue meat out of cans. At the end of the novel, both Lombard and Vera refuse to eat at all, since eating would require returning to the house and risking death. The shift from a fancy dinner to canned meat to no food at all symbolizes the larger pattern of events on the island, as the trappings of civilization gradually fall away and the characters are reduced to mere self-preservation.

SUMMARY & ANALYSIS

CHAPTER 1

SUMMARY: CHAPTER 1

Justice Wargrave, a recently retired judge, is taking a train to the seaside town of Sticklehaven, where he is to catch a boat to Indian Island. He recalls the rumors that have swirled around the island: since a mysterious Mr. Owen purchased the place, people have suggested that a film star or a member of the royal family really owns the island. Wargrave takes a letter from his pocket and glances over its contents. The letter invites him to spend some time on the island and is signed by an old friend of his, Constance Culmington, whom he has not seen for eight years. He reflects that Constance is exactly the kind of woman who would buy a place like Indian Island.

On the same train, Vera Claythorne ponders her invitation to the island. She has been hired as a secretary by Una Nancy Owen, apparently the wife of the island's owner. Vera reflects how lucky she is to get this job, especially after her involvement in a coroner's inquest into someone's death. She was cleared of all blame for the death, we learn, but Hugo Hamilton, the man she loved, thought her guilty. She thinks of the sea and of swimming after someone in particular, knowing she would not reach him in time to save him. She forces her mind away from those memories and glances at the man across from her, thinking he looks well traveled.

The man, Philip Lombard, gazes at Vera and finds her attractive and capable-looking. He has been hired for a mysterious job on Indian Island and is being paid well for it, because he has a reputation as a "good man in a tight place." He has never met his employer; someone named Isaac Morris hired him. Lombard looks forward to whatever he will find on the island.

In another part of the train, Emily Brent sits up straight; she disapproves of slouching. She approves of very little, in fact. She is a very conservative, religious woman who holds most of the world in contempt. She has been invited to Indian Island for a holiday by someone who claims to have once shared a guesthouse with her.

Emily Brent has decided to accept the invitation, even though she cannot quite read the name on the signature.

General Macarthur is taking a slower train to Sticklehaven. He has been invited to the island and promised that some of his friends will be there to talk over old times. He is glad to have the invitation; he has worried that people avoid him because of a thirty-year-old rumor. He does not explain the nature of the rumor.

Dr. Armstrong is driving to the island, having been asked to report on the condition of Mr. Owen's ailing wife. He is a wealthy and successful medical man, but, as he drives, he reflects on the good luck that enabled his career to survive an incident that happened some years before, when he drank heavily. A sports car roars past Armstrong, driven by Tony Marston, a rich, handsome, and carefree young man on his way to Indian Island.

Mr. Blore, a former detective and another guest, is taking a different train from the one the others are taking. He has a list of the names of all the other guests, and he reads it over, reflecting that this job will probably be easy. His only company on the train is an old man who warns him that a storm is coming and that the day of judgment is near. As the man gets off the train, Blore reflects that the old man is closer to death and judgment than he himself is. The narrator warns us that "there, as it happens, he was wrong. . . ."

ANALYSIS: CHAPTER 1

Agatha Christie opens *And Then There Were None* with a shifting point of view unusual in the mystery genre. She gives us a look into each character's thoughts during his or her journey to Sticklehaven and Indian Island. Murder mysteries usually avoid such a tactic—an early glimpse into the murderer's thoughts might reveal his or her guilt and thereby ruin the suspense. In this novel, however, Christie's innovative perspective into different characters' thoughts increases the difficulty of discerning the true murderer and, as a result, establishes a more satisfying ending. For instance, by letting us know what each character is thinking—and such glimpses continue throughout the novel—Christie actually increases the suspense, since each character seems to harbor both innocent and guilty musings, even in the privacy of his or her own thoughts. One of them may be a killer, but we have no way of telling exactly who it is, since man, woman, young, and old alike express suspicious thoughts alongside genuine fears. By the time the killer is revealed, we have run the gamut of responses, from condemnation to sympathy for several characters.

The opening chapter also builds suspense through Christie's use of dramatic irony, the contrast between what a character thinks to be the truth and what we, the readers or audience, know to be the truth. While some of the characters, like Emily Brent and General Macarthur, believe that they are going to Indian Island to visit old friends and others, like Blore and Lombard, believe that they have been hired to do odd jobs on the island, we sense early on that they are all being deceived. The lack of a single reason for the various visitors to come to the island makes the whole process seem like a pretext for some deeper, hidden motive. Because Christie gives us access to her characters' minds, we can see that each character, for the moment, possesses only a limited understanding of the situation, while we can understand that each character is embarking on a greater adventure than he or she realizes.

Christie's partially developed insinuations that her characters possess dark secrets emphasize the suspicious nature of the situation. She reveals nothing definite in these opening scenes, but she gives hints of ugly pasts: Vera recalls being acquitted by a coroner's inquest, which typically takes place after a suspicious death; Lombard thinks about the fact that he has not always followed the law, but "always got away with it"; General Macarthur's thoughts turn to a "damned rumour" that has dogged him for years; Dr. Armstrong thinks about how lucky he has been to "pull himself together" after some "business" years before. Even before the really sinister events begin, we recognize that each potential victim is also a potential suspect.

Christie also establishes a clear authorial presence in the first chapter. She creates a mood of foreboding by using the old seafaring man, who tells Blore that "the day of judgment is at hand." Christie imbues the situation with an even more ominous tone when she explicitly states that Blore is wrong to assume that the old-timer is closer to judgment than he is. This foreshadowing sets a precedent for a significant authorial presence throughout the novel, as Christie repeatedly comments on events in a dramatic or even melodramatic fashion. Because *And Then There Were None* lacks a brilliant detective to serve as an agent of the moral order, the authorial presence must provide omniscient commentary on events.

This kind of heavy-handed writing may be connected to the fact that *And Then There Were None* lacks the brilliant detective who usually plays a central role in murder mysteries. Figures like Sherlock Holmes or Christie's own creations, Miss Marple and Hercule Poirot, typically serve as agents of the moral order, bringing their powers to bear on violent events and thereby investing them with meaning. With no such figure present in this novel, the authorial voice becomes stronger, providing the kind of omniscient commentary on events that a detective usually provides in works of the murder-mystery genre.

CHAPTER 2

SUMMARY: CHAPTER 2

Two taxis wait at the Sticklehaven train station to drive the guests to the dock. Justice Wargrave and Emily Brent share a cab, while Philip Lombard and Vera Claythorne wait together for the second taxi, which cannot leave until General Macarthur arrives on the slower train. The two make small talk until Macarthur's train appears, and then the three of them drive to the dock, where Wargrave and Emily are waiting with a man who introduces himself as "Davis." Just before they set out in the boat, Tony Marston's car appears. In the twilight, he looks like a "a young god" as he drives toward them.

A man named Fred Narracott ferries the group from Sticklehaven to Indian Island. He reflects on what an odd party these guests constitute, since they do not seem to know each other at all and do not seem like friends of a millionaire, which Mr. Owen must be. When the guests arrive at the island, they go up to the house, a large, modern-style building, and are greeted by the butler, Mr. Rogers, and his wife, Mrs. Rogers, who serves as cook and housekeeper. Mr. Rogers tells them that Mr. Owen has been delayed but that they should make themselves at home. Their rooms are prepared, drinks are made, and dinner is on its way.

Each of the guests goes to his or her room. Vera finds her room well appointed. A statue of a bear sits on the mantelpiece, and a nursery rhyme hangs on the wall. Vera recognizes the nursery rhyme from her childhood. In the rhyme, "Ten Little Indians" get killed one by one: the first chokes, the second never wakes up, and so forth until none is left alive. Vera reflects that the poem is appropriate since they are staying on Indian Island. She then looks out at the sea, which makes her think of drowning.

Dr. Armstrong arrives in the evening, passing Wargrave as he goes into the house. He remembers giving medical testimony in front of the judge once or twice, and recalls that Wargrave had a reputation for convincing juries to convict. The two men speak to one another, and Wargrave asks Armstrong about Constance Culmington, who supposedly invited him to the island. He learns that no one by that name is expected. He remarks on the oddity of the host's absence.

Upstairs, Marston takes a bath. Blore ties his tie and notices the "Ten Little Indians" rhyme over his mantelpiece. He resolves not to bungle his job. Macarthur has misgivings about the weekend. He wishes he could leave, but the motorboat has already left. Lombard, coming down for dinner, decides to enjoy the weekend. Upstairs, Emily reads a Bible passage about sinners being judged and cast into hell, and then goes down to dinner.

Analysis: Chapter 2

Having placed her characters in this peculiar situation, Christie seems intent on making each one seem as suspicious as possible. As in the first chapter, she grants us access to the characters' thoughts, but in a way that makes each of them seem slightly sinister—an impression that only increases when we realize that one of them is a murderer. This lack of a single clearly guilty character is one of the ways that *And Then There Were None* subverts the conventions of the traditional mystery story, in which the reader is given a set of clues to work with and can try to solve the case alongside the detective. Christie is not interested in having us solve the case: instead, she seems intent on toying with us, offering plenty of false leads and filling the novel with many potential murderers in order to make it difficult for us to solve the case before the novel's end.

As in the first chapter, the second chapter follows the thoughts of each character in turn. Everyone's musings come across as slightly sinister. Dr. Armstrong, for example, arrives at the island and finds it "magical," and it inspires him to "make plans, fantastic plans"—possibly plans for murder. Tony Marston, in his bath, thinks to himself that he must go through with an unspecified "it," which could refer to the unpleasant weekend or to acts of violence. Mr. Blore, tying his tie, thinks about the "job" he must do, one that he must not bungle. Macarthur wishes he could "make an excuse and get away. . . . Throw up the whole business." He could mean either the business of the weekend or the business of crime. Lombard, coming down for dinner, resembles a beast of prey. He thinks that he will enjoy this weekend, perhaps because he will enjoy preying on others. Finally, Emily Brent reads about the just punishment of sinners with tight-lipped satisfaction, perhaps because she plans to punish sinners herself. With these glimpses we begin to distrust the characters, which makes the mystery more intriguing, more difficult to solve, but ultimately more satisfying to uncover.

This chapter also introduces the "Ten Little Indians" poem, the novel's dominant motif. The use of a childhood nursery rhyme as a schematic model for the murders is one of the novel's most artful touches, since it establishes an atmosphere of dread as the childish verses are transformed into an eerie countdown. The playful verses, then, perversely lead toward the "and then there were none" of the novel's title (the novel's original title was, in fact, *Ten Little Indians*). It is significant that Vera is the first to notice the poem, since it ultimately has the strongest psychological impact on her, eventually driving her to hysterics.

CHAPTERS III–IV

SUMMARY: CHAPTER III

> *Into that silence came The Voice. Without warning, inhuman, penetrating . . . "Ladies and gentlemen! Silence, please . . . You are charged with the following indictments."*
>
> (See QUOTATIONS, p. 49)

The guests enjoy a delicious dinner and begin to relax in spite of the odd circumstances. They notice a set of ten china figures of Indians sitting in the center of the table and immediately associate the figures with the rhyme that hangs framed in all of their rooms. When dinner is over, the whole company moves into the drawing room. Everyone except Mrs. Rogers is in the drawing room when suddenly the group hears a disembodied, mechanical-sounding voice, seemingly coming from nowhere. It accuses each of them of murder, naming the victim and the date of each guest's purported crime. After listing the crimes, it asks if anyone at the bar has something to say in his or her defense.

The voice falls silent, and almost everyone expresses shock and anger. Mrs. Rogers, who has been standing outside the room, faints. While Mr. Rogers goes to fetch her some brandy, everyone else searches for the source of the voice. Eventually, Lombard finds an old-fashioned record player in an adjoining room. Rogers returns and admits to turning it on in accordance with orders from his employer, but he denies knowing what it was going to play. The record is entitled "Swan Song."

Mrs. Rogers revives, and her husband and Dr. Armstrong help her to bed. People pour themselves drinks. When Mr. Rogers returns, he explains that he and his wife have never met their employer, Mr. Owen. He says that an agency hired them, and they received instructions by mail. Everyone else takes turns explaining his or her invitation to the island, and they realize that "Mr. Owen" impersonated various old friends and specific acquaintances in the letters. Judge Wargrave, who has taken charge of the discussion, notes that the recorded message mentioned a Mr. Blore, but not a "Mr. Davis," the name Blore has chosen as an alias. Blore then reveals his real name and admits that he was hired via post as a private detective to protect the jewels of Mrs. U. N. Owen. Wargrave suggests that U. N. Owen sounds like and stands for "unknown," and that a homicidal maniac has invited them all here.

SUMMARY: CHAPTER IV

The subject turns to the accusations made by the voice on the record, and the guests defend themselves. Wargrave, accused of killing a man named Edward Seton, says that Seton was an accused murderer on whom he passed sentence. Armstrong, remembering the case, privately recalls that everyone felt sure Seton would be acquitted, but Wargrave influenced the jury, which found Seton guilty. Vera, accused of killing Cyril Hamilton, tells the group that she was his governess, and he drowned while swimming to a rock. She says she tried her best to save him. Macarthur, accused of killing his wife's lover, Arthur Richmond, says that Richmond was one of his officers who died on a routine reconnaissance mission; Macarthur denies that his wife ever had an affair. Lombard, accused of killing twenty-one members of an East African tribe, admits to taking their food and abandoning them in the wilderness, saying that he did so in order to save himself. Tony Marston, accused of killing John and Lucy Combes, remarks that they must have been two children he ran over by accident.

Mr. Rogers says that he and his wife did not kill Jennifer Brady, their employer, an old, sickly woman who died one night when Mr. Rogers could not reach the doctor in time. He admits that they inherited some money after her death. Blore says that when he was a police inspector, he testified against a man named James Landor in a bank robbery case. Landor later died in jail, but Blore insists that Landor was guilty. Armstrong, accused of causing the death of a woman named Louisa Mary Clees, denies knowing the name but privately remembers the case. Clees was an elderly woman on whom he operated while drunk. Only the dignified Emily Brent will not speak to the accusation made against her.

Wargrave suggests they leave in the morning as soon as the boat arrives; all the guests but one concur. Tony Marston suggests they ought to stay and solve the case. He then takes a drink, chokes on it, and dies.

ANALYSIS: CHAPTERS III–IV

The truth about the party on the island is now partially revealed, since the recorded voice clarifies the hints that Christie has dropped so far about her characters' shady pasts. Now we know that they not only all have secrets, but that they have all committed murder in one form or another. We also learn that their host, whoever he or she may be, has a dark sense of humor and delights in tricks and word games. The name "U. N. Owen," or, as Wargrave translates it, "unknown," is a play on words. Additionally, the title of the record that announces their crimes is "Swan Song," a term that refers to the sweet song supposedly sung by dying swans. The host's central and most perverse word game involves the "Ten Little Indians" poem, as becomes apparent after a few murders have taken place.

Most of the guests stoutly deny the accusations made against them. As the novel progresses, however, these early denials begin to break down under the strain of the situation, and one after another the characters admit their guilt to each other. It is telling to watch, in Chapter IV, the way each deals with the allegations against him or her. Most of the guests deny the charges, but the ones who do so the loudest, we realize, are actually the people most wracked with guilt. We see earlier how Vera, Macarthur, and Armstrong, for example, are haunted by memories of their crimes but now claim to be innocent.

Meanwhile, the people who seem to feel no guilt over their alleged crimes manifest different reactions. Lombard, who throughout the novel never displays remorse for anything, willingly admits to leaving men to die in the wilderness. He sees no problem with having self-preservation as his highest value. Similarly, Tony Marston readily owns up to running down the children. A complete egotist, he seems to regard the incident chiefly as an inconvenience for himself, since his license was suspended. Emily Brent, for her part, refuses even to speak about her incident, which reflects her intense sense of propriety but also her powerful conviction of her own righteousness. She is not a criminal, her mind tells her, but virtuous and pure, and so there is no reason to even bother denying the charges, which she finds too ridiculous to trouble her.

The self-righteousness of some of the characters reflects their position in the social hierarchy. Emily Brent does not care about the death of her former maid partly because her maid is not her social equal. Similarly, the attractive and youthful Tony Marston inhabits the top tier of the social hierarchy; he is wealthy and frivolous, and feels no remorse for killing children who live in what he describes as "some cottage or other." Those on society's lower tiers behave more meekly in the face of the accusations. Mr. Rogers, for example, continues to perform his duties as butler even after Mrs. Rogers has fainted and she and her husband have been accused of murder. Even as the situation on the island deteriorates, constricting social hierarchies prevail.

CHAPTERS V–VI

SUMMARY: CHAPTER V

Armstrong examines the drink and finds it was poisoned, but since Marston poured it himself, the guests assume he committed suicide. Still, they find it hard to believe that such a high-spirited young man would want to take his own life. Marston's body is carried to his bedroom and placed beneath a sheet. After a time, everyone goes upstairs to bed except for Rogers, who stays downstairs to clean up. As they enter their rooms, each guest locks his or her door. The house, so modern and gleaming, now seems horrifying in its blankness.

As he prepares for bed, Wargrave thinks about Edward Seton, the man whom the voice earlier accused him of sentencing to death. The defense defended Seton well, and the prosecution presented a poor case. Everyone assumed the jury would acquit Seton. Wargrave smiles, remembering how during his summing up "[h]e'd cooked Seton's goose." Downstairs, Rogers notices that although ten little Indian statues originally sat on the table, now there are only nine. Macarthur lies awake in bed, recalling how during World War I he discovered that his young wife was having an affair with one of his officers. Furious, he ordered the officer, Richmond, on an impossible mission, effectively sending him to his death. No one suspected him at the time, except perhaps one of the other officers, a man named Armitage. His wife became distant and died of pneumonia a few years later. Macarthur retired and lived by the sea, but after a time he began to worry, suspecting that Armitage had spread the story around and that people knew his secret. Now, lying in his bedroom listening to the sound of the sea, a strange feeling of peace comes over him, and he realizes that he does not really want to leave the island.

In her bedroom, Vera remembers her time as Cyril's governess. She was in love with Cyril Hamilton's cousin, Hugo, but Hugo was too poor to marry her and support both himself and her. Vera knew that if Cyril died, Hugo would inherit the family fortune. One day Cyril begged her again and again to be allowed to swim to a rock in the ocean. Vera pushes these recollections aside. As she passes the mantelpiece, she notices the similarity between Marston's death and the first verse of the "Ten Little Indians" poem, which reads, "One choked his little self and then there were nine."

Summary: Chapter VI

Armstrong has a nightmare in which he stands at his operating table, realizing he must kill the patient on the table. The patient looks like Emily Brent, then like Marston. Rogers, worried because he cannot rouse his wife, comes into the room and wakes Armstrong. Armstrong rises and goes to find that Mrs. Rogers has died in her sleep, perhaps of an overdose of sleeping pills. Rogers says she took only the pills Armstrong gave her.

In the morning the guests rise, hoping to catch sight of the boat back to the mainland. Vera, Lombard, and Blore go to the summit of the island to watch for it, but it doesn't appear. After breakfast, Armstrong announces Mrs. Rogers's death to the group. The group is alarmed, and Macarthur gives Rogers his condolences when he returns to the room. When Rogers leaves the room, the group begins to speculate about the cause of his wife's death. Emily Brent insists it was an act of God and that Mrs. Rogers died of a guilty conscience after hearing the recorded accusation of murder the previous night. Blore suggests that Rogers killed his wife in the hopes of covering up their secret.

After the meal, Blore and Lombard discuss their situation on the terrace and decide that the boat will not come. Macarthur, passing them, expresses his agreement in a dazed voice and wanders off, saying that none of them will ever leave the island. Meanwhile, a baffled and frightened Rogers shows Armstrong that only eight Indian figures remain on the table.

ANALYSIS: CHAPTERS V–VI

While *And Then There Were None* is a classic of detective fiction, it can also be seen as a forerunner of the modern horror or slasher story, with its almost supernatural overtones and the strange, serial killer–like murderer. And like a horror movie, the novel depends, both for suspense and for the working out of its plot, on foolish behavior by the killer's victims. In these chapters, we see the guests repeatedly fail to grasp what should be obvious—namely, that Marston's death could not have been a suicide and so must have been a murder. Because they refuse to admit this possibility, they are not on their guard, and the murderer easily disposes of Mrs. Rogers. Even once the characters realize what is going on, they continue to make obvious blunders, such as going places alone, that leave them vulnerable.

Part of this blundering seems to stem from a mistaken devotion to propriety and class distinctions. Even after his wife's death, for instance, Rogers is still expected to serve as the butler and housekeeper, and he does so without objecting and without even showing much grief. The upper-class characters think nothing of discussing Rogers behind his back, with Blore going so far as to accuse him of murder. Eventually, Rogers's devotion to his duties as a butler provides the murderer with an opportunity to finish him off.

During the night following Marston's death, meanwhile, Christie uses her typical brief glimpses into characters' minds to provide more information about their crimes. We learn the details of how Macarthur murdered his wife's lover, for instance. At the same time, Macarthur is somewhat removed from suspicion, since his thoughts are manifestly not those of a murderer. Perhaps Christie exonerates him because he is about to die; indeed, his sudden, strange urge never to leave the island foreshadows his death the next morning. Meanwhile, Vera's thoughts reveal how she went about disposing of her ward, Cyril, and why she did it, while Wargrave's thoughts reveal only that he feels righteous about the execution of Edward Seton. Armstrong's hallucinatory dream suggests rather heavy-handedly that he has a guilty conscience about the woman who died on his operating table. It also serves to plant suspicion in our minds: since Armstrong is dreaming about killing his fellow guests, perhaps he is planning to kill them for real.

A number of brief scenes in these chapters foreshadow later events. Just before Rogers brings him news of the missing figurine, for example, Armstrong emerges onto the terrace and tries to decide whether he wants to consult with Wargrave or with Lombard and Blore. He turns toward Wargrave, foreshadowing his later, foolish alliance with the judge. Also, the moment when Blore, Lombard, and Vera congregate at the summit of the island to await the boat foreshadows the end of the novel, when they are the only three left alive, and they again gather at the island's summit. Meanwhile, the motif of the "Ten Little Indians" poem continues to be developed, with the disappearance of the figurines and the correspondence between the deaths and the verses of the rhyme. Again, it is Vera who notices the connection between the poem and the death of Marston, foreshadowing the effect that the verses later have on her fragile psyche.

CHAPTERS VII–VIII

SUMMARY: CHAPTER VII

Emily and Vera take a walk together. Emily reiterates her conviction that Mrs. Rogers died of a guilty conscience. She tells Vera the story of Beatrice Taylor, the girl the recorded voice accused Emily of kill-ing. Beatrice Taylor worked for Emily as a maid, but when Beatrice got pregnant, Emily immediately threw her out of the house. Friend-less and despairing, Beatrice drowned herself. Emily insists that she has no reason to feel remorse, but the story horrifies Vera.

Meanwhile, Lombard and Armstrong consult with each other. They discuss the possibility that Rogers killed his wife, and Arm-strong expresses his conviction that the Rogers couple probably did kill the old woman in their care simply by withholding drugs that she needed. They also consider the possibility that Mrs. Rogers killed herself, but two deaths—hers and Marston's—within twelve hours seems like an improbable coincidence. Armstrong tells Lombard that two Indian figures have disappeared. When Armstrong recites the first two verses of the poem, Lombard notices that they neatly correspond to the two murders. They decide that their host, Mr. Owen, committed the murders and is now hiding on the island, and they determine to search for him.

SUMMARY: CHAPTER VIII

Joined by Blore, Armstrong and Lombard make an exhaustive sweep of the small island. Since the island is mostly bare rock, few places for concealment exist. It turns out that Lombard has a revolver, which surprises Blore. As they make their search, the men come across a dazed Macarthur sitting by himself, staring off into the sea. He tells them that there is very little time and that they need to leave him alone. They decide that he must be crazy. Leaving him, they discuss how they might signal the mainland, and Lombard points out that a storm is brewing, which will isolate them. He adds that the fishermen and village people probably have been told (by Mr. Owen, presumably) to disregard all signals from the island. The men come to some cliffs they want to search for caves, but they need a rope. Blore returns to the house to get one, while Armstrong wonders about Macarthur's apparent madness. Meanwhile, Vera goes out for a walk and comes across the Macarthur. She sits down, and he talks of the impending end of his life and of the relief he feels, given the guilt he has felt over the death of Richmond. Eventually, having seemingly become unaware of Vera's presence, he begins to murmur the name of his dead wife as if he expects her to appear.

When Blore returns with a rope, he finds only Armstrong, who is musing that Macarthur may be the killer. Lombard returns, having gone to check some unnamed theory, and climbs down the cliff to make his search for caves. As Armstrong and Blore hold the rope, Blore remarks that Lombard climbs extremely well. He says he does not trust Lombard and thinks it odd that he brought a revolver, saying, "It's only in books that people carry revolvers around as a matter of course." Lombard finds nothing on the cliff face, and the three men return to the house, where they make a thorough search for their missing host. The search goes quickly, since the modern house contains few potential hiding places. They hear someone moving about upstairs in Mrs. Rogers's bedroom, where her body has been laid, but it turns out to be Mr. Rogers. Completing their search, they conclude there is no one on the island but the eight of them.

ANALYSIS: CHAPTERS VII–VIII

We are finally given an account of Emily Brent's crime in the form of a remarkably honest confession from her own mouth. She makes an interesting case, since, in a certain way, she is less explicitly guilty of murder than most of the other guests. After all, her only action was to turn a pregnant girl out of her home: she did not intend to kill Beatrice Taylor the way Vera intended to kill Cyril or Macarthur intended to kill Richmond, his wife's lover. Nor did Emily directly cause someone's death, as did Armstrong and Marston. Nevertheless, Christie depicts Emily as the most unsympathetic character in the novel, less for what she did than for her utter lack of remorse and unbending faith in her own righteousness. The others may have committed worse crimes, but at least they admit to themselves that they did indeed commit crimes. Emily Brent has no such consciousness of her own guilt. She is, as Christie puts it, "encased in her own armour of virtue," using her religious values to justify her actions.

Meanwhile, some of the characters begin to realize the truth about the situation and the danger they are all in while they inhabit an island with a crazed murderer. In particular, we see the three younger men—Armstrong, Blore, and Lombard—begin to work together in an effort to solve the mystery. Armstrong and Lombard make the connection between the poem, the deaths, and the missing figurines, which enables them for the first time to grasp the murderer's overall plan. Then, deciding to search the island, they turn to Blore to provide muscle. This grouping of three seems like a strong alliance, bringing together Armstrong's intelligence, Lombard's cunning, and Blore's police experience. Indeed, these three men end up, along with Vera, the last surviving guests. The murderer appears to be weeding out the weaker characters first: Marston, self-absorbed and overconfident, dies first, followed by the fainting Mrs. Rogers. Macarthur's increased detachment from the world, manifested in his odd behavior during these chapters, makes him an easy target for the murderer. That the strongest characters survive prepares us for a heightening of events, since the murderer will no doubt have to be savvy to kill them off.

Unfortunately for Blore, Armstrong, and Lombard, mutual suspicion compromises their alliance, as each man suspects that one of the others is the killer. We can already see this suspicion developing during their search of the island, when Blore asks Armstrong why Lombard happens to be carrying a revolver. Blore's mistrust of Lombard grows as the novel progresses, and it comes out into the open once they are the only two men left alive. But, as Vera points out later, Lombard's personality—he is a man of action primarily interested in saving his own life—makes him totally wrong for the part of a murderer whose primary goal seems to be the delivery of cosmic justice. But Blore does not consider this idea, because his policeman's mind is limited. Blore's folly is another example of how Christie subverts the conventions of the detective story. The former policeman is the closest thing to a detective on the island, yet, unlike an almost omniscient, Sherlock Holmes–style sleuth, Blore never manages to get things right.

CHAPTERS IX–X

SUMMARY: CHAPTER IX

> *Mr. Owen could only come to the island in one way. It is perfectly clear. Mr. Owen is one of us.*
> (See QUOTATIONS, p. 50)

Blore, Lombard, and Armstrong become argumentative. Blore suggests that Armstrong gave Mrs. Rogers an overdose of sleeping medication either by accident or on purpose. Lombard tells Blore not to be offensive, and Blore demands to know why Lombard carries a gun. Lombard explains that he was hired to do a job by Isaac Morris, who implied that he might find trouble of some sort on the island. The bell rings, announcing lunch. Everyone troops in for the midday meal except for Macarthur, whom Armstrong goes to fetch. Rogers serves a makeshift lunch of cold ham and tongue along with a few other items, anxiously expressing his hope that the food will satisfy the guests. People make small talk about the approaching storm and then hear the doctor returning at a run. He bursts into the dining room, and Vera immediately surmises aloud that Macarthur is dead. Armstrong confirms this fear, stating that Macarthur was killed by a blow to the head. Blore and Armstrong retrieve Macarthur's body, and the storm breaks as they bear the corpse into the house and place it in Macarthur's room. Vera and Rogers notice that only seven statues remain on the dining-room table.

Everyone except Rogers gathers in the drawing room, and Wargrave takes charge of the meeting. He says he has come to the conclusion that the murderer is one of the guests. The others, except for Vera, agree with this theory. He then asks if anyone can be cleared of suspicion. After some initial objections, including discussions of whether women and professional men can possibly be suspected of such crimes, it is agreed that they must proceed as if any of them could be the murderer. The guests then review their movements of the past two days to see if anyone's actions made it logistically impossible that he or she committed all three murders. No one has a foolproof alibi. Wargrave warns everyone to be on his or her guard, and dismisses them as if adjourning a court.

SUMMARY: CHAPTER X

Vera and Lombard talk in the living room. They agree that they do not suspect one another. Lombard remarks that Vera seems very level-headed for a woman. He then tells her that he suspects Wargrave; perhaps, Lombard suggests, years of playing God as a judge have driven him mad and made him want to be both judge and executioner. Vera says she suspects Armstrong, because two deaths by poison sounds like a doctor's handiwork. She suggests that he might have killed Macarthur when he went down to fetch him for lunch. She also points out that since Armstrong is the only member of the group with medical knowledge, he can say what he likes about the manner of death and no one can contradict him.

Rogers, polishing the silver, asks Blore if he has any suspicions. Blore says he suspects someone, but he will not say whom. Meanwhile, Wargrave and Armstrong talk. Wargrave strikes Armstrong as eager to hold on to his life. Armstrong worries that they will all be murdered in their beds, and Wargrave thinks to himself that Armstrong can think only in clichés and that he has a "thoroughly commonplace mind." Wargrave then says that while he has no evidence that would stand up in a court of law, he thinks he knows the identity of the murderer.

Emily sits in her room, writing in her diary. She begins to feel groggy and writes in a shaky hand that the murderer is Beatrice Taylor (the pregnant maid she once employed who killed herself). She snaps to her senses and cannot believe she could have written such a thing. She thinks that she must be going mad.

Later that afternoon, everyone gathers in the drawing room. The normalcy of teatime makes them relax a bit. Rogers rushes in to announce that a bathroom curtain made of scarlet oilsilk has gone missing. No one knows what this absence means, but everyone feels nervous again. The guests eat a dinner consisting mostly of canned food. They retire to bed soon after eating, locking their doors behind them. Only Rogers remains downstairs. Before he goes to bed, he locks the dining-room door so that no one can remove any of the remaining Indian figures during the night.

ANALYSIS: CHAPTERS IX–X

The storm that breaks as the men carry Macarthur's body inside symbolizes the increasing gravity of the situation on Indian Island. The guests can no longer deny that something terrible is afoot, and the windswept island begins to seem like a prison. Amid this turmoil, Wargrave takes charge, bringing the surviving characters together to confront the menace facing them all. His suggestion that the murderer is one of them forces the remaining guests to confront suspicions and convictions they are earlier unwilling to face. Here Wargrave plays the role of the conventional murder-mystery detective, gathering evidence, drawing conclusions, and making cryptic comments, such as his remark to Armstrong that the identity of the murderer is "clearly indicated" by the evidence. Indeed, most of Christie's mysteries end with a scene much like the group discussion in Chapter IX, in which the detective gathers the suspects together, reviews the evidence, and announces the identity of the killer. The formula gets tweaked in *And Then There Were None,* with the climactic and orderly drawing-room scene coming halfway through the novel and the identity of the murderer remaining unknown.

Throughout the novel, Christie depicts the weaknesses of each character, weaknesses that eventually doom them. For instance, we earlier see how Vera, more than the others, is plagued by guilt over her crime. In the group discussion in Chapter IX, the weaknesses of Armstrong and Lombard become apparent. Armstrong declares that he is a "well-known professional man" and so should be exempt from suspicion. He is blinded, in other words, by ideas of class and respectability; he cannot imagine that any "professional" person could be a murderer. This attitude makes him suspect Lombard, since Lombard is far from respectable, and prevents him from suspecting others. Lombard has a similarly limited understanding of the world—his quaint and antiquated view of women makes him unable to fathom that the killer could be female. "I suppose you'll leave the women out of it," he tells Wargrave, and later, in his conversation with Vera, he tells her that she is too "sane" and "level-headed" to be the killer. Lombard has an old-fashioned, almost chivalrous view of women as powerless and harmless, which leads him to a fatal underestimation of Vera.

Christie uses the details of everyday life to illustrate the increasing desperation of the situation. The first night, the guests eat a sumptuous meal; now, however, they eat cold tongue. They begin to watch each other suspiciously until their bedroom doors are safely locked for the night, and they openly express their misgivings about one another. The tense situation is chipping away at their standards of decorum. Still, strangely enough, Rogers continues his impeccable service, staying downstairs to clean up after everyone and scraping meals together as best he can. Even though his wife has been murdered and there is a murderer on the loose, he does not find his continued subservience strange, and neither do the guests. His determination to cling to his place in the social hierarchy proves a fatal weakness, since the class divisions that separate him from the guests make him an easy target for the murderer.

Chapters XI–XII

Summary: Chapter XI

> *Oh, don't you understand? Haven't you read that idiotic rhyme?. . . Seven little Indian boys chopping up sticks.*
>
> (See QUOTATIONS, p. 51)

Lombard sleeps late. Waking, he wonders why Rogers did not come to rouse him earlier. He finds the others, except for Emily. Blore and Wargrave have to be roused from sleep. Downstairs, they find no sign of Rogers. Emily comes in wearing a raincoat, saying that she has been walking around the island. Entering the dining room, Vera discovers, to everyone's horror, that another statue is missing. They soon find Rogers's body in the woodshed, with a hatchet wound in the back of his neck. Vera suffers a slight breakdown, raving about how the rhyme has been fulfilled—"One chopped himself in halves, and then there were six." The next verse pertains to bees, and she asks hysterically if there are any hives on the island. Armstrong slaps her, and she comes to her senses.

The group breaks up while Emily and Vera prepare breakfast. Blore tells Lombard that he thinks Emily is the killer. After some prodding, Blore admits to Lombard that he testified against an innocent man. As she cooks breakfast, Vera stares off into space, letting the bacon burn while she remembers Cyril disappearing into the water. Emily remains outwardly calm, but when Vera asks her if she is afraid to die, Emily begins to get nervous. She thinks to herself that she will not die because she has led an upright life. At breakfast, the remaining guests behave very politely, but frantic thoughts flood their minds.

SUMMARY: CHAPTER XII

After breakfast, Wargrave suggests they convene in half an hour to discuss the situation. Emily feels woozy, so she remains at the table. Armstrong offers to give her a sedative, but she recoils at the idea. As the others go out and clean up in the kitchen, Emily sees a bee buzzing outside of the window and realizes that there is someone behind her. She seems drugged or delusional; she thinks sluggishly and calmly of bees and of how much she likes honey. She thinks the person in the room is Beatrice Taylor, dripping with water from the river. She then feels a prick on her neck.

In the drawing room, Blore says he thinks Emily is the killer. Vera tells them the story of Beatrice Taylor. Some seem to agree with Blore's theory, but Wargrave points out that they have no evidence. They go to the dining room to get Emily and find her dead, her skin turning blue. They notice the bee buzzing outside and remember the rhyme: "A bumblebee stung one and then there were five." Emily apparently died of an injection from a hypodermic syringe. Armstrong admits that he has a syringe in his medical bag. The remaining guests go together to search his room, and they find the syringe has vanished.

Wargrave suggests they lock away any potential weapons, including Lombard's gun and Armstrong's medicine case. Lombard reluctantly agrees, but when they go to his bedroom they find that his revolver is missing. At Wargrave's prompting, everyone strips (Vera puts on a bathing suit) and is searched for weapons. They store all potentially lethal drugs in a case that requires a key. The case is placed in a chest that requires a different key. Wargrave gives one key to Lombard and one to Blore. This way the two strong men would have to fight one another if one wanted the other's key, and neither could break into the case or chest without making a great racket. The group searches for Lombard's gun but cannot find it. They do find the doctor's syringe, however; it was thrown out the dining-room window, along with the sixth Indian figure.

ANALYSIS: CHAPTERS XI–XII

Christie continues her tactic of casting suspicion on a variety of characters. In the moments following Rogers's death, it is Emily who seems the most likely suspect. She possesses the kind of religious mania that might drive someone to kill in the name of justice, and the fact that she is out walking when Rogers is killed gives her an opportunity to commit the murder. Blore, displaying his usual habit of jumping to conclusions, becomes the champion of her guilt. But, of course, no sooner does Christie make us suspect Emily than she briskly removes Emily from suspicion by having her killed off.

The killer's success with Rogers and Emily depends on their own mistakes as much as upon the killer's cleverness. Rogers, as we see earlier, stubbornly refuses to alter his routine, even in these bizarre circumstances. He continues to perform his butler chores, washing up after people, remaining downstairs to clean up after the others have gone to bed, and rising early in the morning and going out alone to chop firewood. By carrying on as if the situation is normal, he separates himself from the group. This isolation casts suspicion on him, but it also enables the murderer to make short work of him. In the same way, Emily refuses to take the kind of precautions that the others are taking: she gets up early and goes walking alone, and then after breakfast she sits alone in the dining room, presenting an inviting target for the killer. The deaths of Rogers and Emily drive home the point that separation from the larger group is fatal.

Although we learn almost nothing about the characters who die early in the novel, we know much about the characters that remain. Clear dynamics have emerged by this point: Blore and Lombard are rivals, with Lombard clearly the more resourceful of the two. Wargrave, meanwhile, has managed to establish himself in a leadership role, with the others following his advice, as when they strip and search each other and when they lock away the medicines. Vera, who behaves as if she trusts Lombard more than the others, is the only woman still surviving, which suggests that she possesses unsuspected resources. Her weakness, though, is demonstrated again in her hysterical reaction to Rogers's death, when she is easily affected and emotionally undone by suggestive, seemingly supernatural devices such as the "Ten Little Indians" poem. Armstrong, finally, is the most nervous and high-strung of the group, and he is a focus of suspicion, both from Vera and from Blore.

In these chapters, Christie makes use of a new authorial tactic, recording characters' thoughts without identifying the thinker. As the guests sit around at breakfast, we hear a succession of nervous thoughts, including a few suspicious ones ("Would it work? I wonder. It's worth trying," and "The damned fool, he believed every word I said to him. It was easy"). All we know is that one or more characters are plotting to mislead others, confusing our understanding of the events on the island.

CHAPTERS XIII–XIV

SUMMARY: CHAPTER XIII

> *Armstrong raised the limp hand. . . . He said—and his voice was expressionless, dead, far away: "He's been shot . . . "*
>
> (See QUOTATIONS, p. 52)

The uneasy group sits in the drawing room. Armstrong seems particularly nervous; he lights cigarette after cigarette with shaky hands. The guests use candles, since Rogers is no longer around to operate the house's generator. Vera offers to make tea, and the other four go with her to watch her make it. They tacitly agree that only one person will go anywhere at a time, while the other four stay together.

Later, Vera gets up to take a shower. She enters her room and suddenly feels as if she were again at the seashore where Cyril drowned. She smells the salt of the sea, and the wind blows out her candle. She feels something wet and clammy touch her throat, and screams. The men rush to the rescue and find that it was a piece of seaweed hanging from the ceiling that scared her. Lombard thinks it was meant to frighten her to death. Blore fetches a glass of alcohol, and they feud over whether he might have poisoned it. Suddenly, they notice that Wargrave is not with them. They hurry downstairs, and find him sitting in a chair, dressed in the red curtain that was missing and a gray judge's wig made from some wool that Emily had lost. Armstrong inspects Wargrave and says that he has been shot in the head. Wargrave's body is carried to his room. Again, everyone notices the similarity to the "Ten Little Indians" poem: "Five little Indian boys going in for law; one got in Chancery [dressed like a judge] and then there were four."

SUMMARY: CHAPTER XIV

The remaining four eat canned tongue for dinner and then go to bed. Everyone thinks he or she now knows the killer's identity, although no one makes an accusation aloud. Entering his room, Lombard notes that his gun is back in its drawer. Vera lies awake, tormented by memories of Cyril's drowning. She recalls telling him he could swim out to the rock, knowing that he would be unable to make it and would drown. She wonders if Hugo knows what she did. Vera notices a hook in the ceiling and realizes that the seaweed must have hung from it. For some reason, the black hook fascinates her.

Lying in bed, Blore tries to go over the facts of the case in his head, but his thoughts keep returning to his framing of Landor. He hears a noise outside. He listens at the door and hears it again. Slipping outside into the hall, he sees a figure going downstairs and out the front door. Blore checks the rooms and finds that Armstrong is not in his room. He wakes Lombard and Vera. The two men tell Vera to remain in her room, and they hurry outside to investigate. In her room, Vera thinks she hears the sound of breaking glass and then stealthy footsteps moving in the house. Blore and Lombard return without finding anyone: the island is empty, and Armstrong seems to have vanished. In the house they find a broken windowpane and only three Indian figurines in the dining room.

ANALYSIS: CHAPTERS XIII–XIV

The death of Wargrave and the disappearance of Armstrong mark the novel's climax. Although neither we nor the remaining characters realize it at this juncture, Wargrave is not dead; rather, he and Armstrong have conspired to fake his death. Armstrong does not suspect Wargrave, largely because of Wargrave's place in society, and this trust reflects Armstrong's fatal obsession with social status. He thinks that the trick of faking Wargrave's death will confuse the murderer and flush him out into the open. Instead, it leads to Armstrong's own death and fundamentally changes the murderer's relationship to the rest of the group. Before these chapters, Wargrave is simply part of the group, one suspect among many. Now, his place on the island has changed, since everyone else (except for Armstrong, his co-conspirator) believes him to be dead. His deceit makes him more vulnerable, in a sense, since if anyone catches a glimpse of him moving around the island, his guilt will be obvious. At the same time, however, no one else is even aware that he is alive, which increases his freedom of action dramatically. He can do as he pleases, and, as long as he returns to his room undetected and pretends to be dead, no one will even suspect him.

Of course, our understanding of these climactic scenes is complicated by the fact that their crucial events are hidden from us. Christie leaves us in the same situation as the remaining guests—Blore, Vera, and Lombard—which dramatically increases the suspense of the narrative. From this point onward, the murders seem to defy rational explanation. For instance, Armstrong vanishes from the island while everyone else is asleep. The deeds of the murderer thus take on an almost supernatural quality, one that is heightened by their continued correspondence to the "Ten Little Indians" poem. One of the obvious themes of Christie's novel is the working out of justice, since all the murder victims are being punished for earlier crimes. As the novel nears its end, this justice seems to be delivered not by any human agent, but by some supernatural power, as if a vengeful God is doling out punishment.

Christie's decision to leave us in the dark about Wargrave's faked death also marks the moment when she irrevocably violates the rules of the detective-fiction genre. Typically, a detective story offers a set of clues that readers can use to solve the case for themselves. By withholding the crucial information about Wargrave's seeming death, however, Christie makes the case practically impossible to solve.

Chapters XV–XVI

Summary: Chapter XV

The remaining three eat breakfast. The storm is gone, and they feel as though a nightmare has passed. Lombard begins to make plans to signal the mainland. They discuss Armstrong's mysterious disappearance, and Lombard and Blore get into an argument: Blore finds it sinister that Lombard has his revolver again, but Lombard refuses to give it up. Blore suggests that Lombard may be the killer, and Lombard asks why he wouldn't simply shoot Blore if he were the murderer. Vera scolds them for being distracted. She points out the verse in the rhyme that applies to Armstrong's death: "A red herring swallowed one and then there were three." A "red herring" is a term for a false lead or a decoy, and she thinks that Armstrong is not really dead and that he has tricked them somehow. Blore points out that the next line is about a zoo, which the murderer will have a difficult time enacting on their island, but Vera says impatiently that they are turning into animals.

Vera, Blore, and Lombard spend the morning on the cliffs trying to signal a distress message to the coast using a mirror, but they get no answer. They decide to stay outside to avoid the danger of the house, but eventually Blore wants to fetch something to eat. He is nervous about going alone, but Lombard refuses to lend him the revolver. When Blore is gone, Lombard tries to convince Vera that Blore is probably the killer. Vera says she thinks Armstrong must still be alive. She then suggests that the killer could be alien or supernatural. Lombard thinks this mention of the supernatural indicates Vera's troubled conscience and asks her if she did kill Cyril. She vehemently denies it at first, but when he asks if a man was involved, she feels exhausted and admits that there was a man involved. They hear a faint crash from the house and go to investigate. Blore has been crushed by something thrown from Vera's window: the bear-shaped marble clock that stood on her mantle. Thinking that Armstrong must be inside the house somewhere, the two go to wait for help. On their way to the cliffs, they see something on the beach below. They climb down to look and there find Armstrong's body.

SUMMARY: CHAPTER XVI

Vera and Lombard, dazed, stand over Armstrong's body. Vera looks at Lombard and sees his wolflike face and sharp teeth. Lombard nastily says that the end has come. Vera suggests they move the body above the water line. Lombard sneers at her, but agrees. When they are finished, Lombard realizes something is wrong and wheels around to find Vera pointing his revolver at him. She has picked it from his pocket. He decides to gamble and lunges at her; she automatically pulls the trigger and Lombard falls to the ground, shot through the heart.

Vera feels an enormous wave of relief and severe exhaustion. She heads back to the house to get some sleep before help arrives. As she enters the house, she sees the three statues on the table. She breaks two of them and picks the third up, trying to remember the last line of the poem. She thinks it is "He got married and then there were none." She begins to think of Hugo, the man she loved but lost as a result of Cyril's drowning. At the top of the stairs she drops the revolver without noticing what she does. She feels sure that Hugo is waiting for her upstairs. When she opens the door of her bedroom, she sees a noose hanging from the black hook that previously held the seaweed. She sees that Hugo wants her to hang herself, and then she remembers the real last line of the poem: "He went and hanged himself and then there were none." Without a second thought she puts her head in the noose and kicks away the chair.

ANALYSIS: CHAPTERS XV–XVI

The apparent end of the novel is calculated to leave us in a state of utter confusion. Since we have no idea that Wargrave is still alive, it seems that the murderer must either be Vera or Lombard. Yet we are left with no idea how either one could possibly have killed Blore, whose death takes place while the two are together by the sea, or, for that matter, how either could have killed Armstrong, since both of them are asleep in the house when he goes outside. Additionally, there is the matter of the Indian figurines, which continue to disappear like clockwork even when the house is apparently empty.

When all of these facts are considered, the only possible conclusion is the correct one—namely, that someone else is still alive on the island. Yet all the evidence that the novel has provided thus far suggests that this is impossible. In their final confrontation, both Vera and Lombard accept it as a given that they are alone on Indian Island, and each assumes that the other is the killer. In a way, their behavior is irrational, since they should know that neither one of them could possibly have killed Blore. This kind of perfect rationality, however, may be too much to ask of a pair of human beings who have endured such a strange and terrible sequence of events. In the end, both Lombard and Vera accept the logic of the poem, and they assume that everyone who seems to have died really is dead. A careful examination of the evidence is beyond their capabilities.

The final three characters die in ways consistent with what Christie shows us of their respective personalities. Blore, who proves himself bold but blundering, dies because he is foolhardy enough to return to the house alone. Lombard, who harbors a deep-seated sense of women as a harmless sex, dies because he underestimates Vera's capabilities—first by putting her in a position to steal his gun and then, when he lunges at her, by assuming that she won't be capable of shooting him. Finally, Vera is haunted by guilt about Cyril Hamilton's death. She remembers the events with a nearly hallucinogenic clarity, smelling seawater and seeing moonlight. Additionally, she is powerfully affected by the "Ten Little Indians" poem and has a horrified fascination with the hook hanging from the ceiling of her bedroom. All of these traits come together, exacerbating the enormous shock of being responsible for someone's death. Unable to cope, Vera falls into a kind of trance and gives in to the fate that she believes she cannot escape.

This combination of guilt, stress, and the supernatural suggestiveness of the poem might not really be enough to drive someone to suicide. But, however believable we find this last scene, the novel clearly intends it to be a realistic picture of an individual undone by guilt over her own actions. *And Then There Were None* is a murder mystery in which none of the victims is innocent, and in which most of them are plagued by feelings of guilt and remorse. Vera's suicide—which parallels Macarthur's earlier decision to sit by the sea waiting to die—is thus a fitting end to a novel that revolves around the administration of justice. Vera knows that she is guilty, and so, with Wargrave having set the stage, she administers justice to herself.

Epilogue

Summary: Epilogue

> I have wanted—let me admit it frankly—to commit a
> murder myself. . . . I was, or could be, an artist in
> crime!
>
> (See QUOTATIONS, p. 53)

Two policeman, Sir Thomas Legge and Inspector Maine, discuss the perplexing Indian Island case. They have reconstructed much of what happened on Indian Island from diaries kept by various guests. It is clear to them that the murderer was not Blore, Lombard, or Vera. When they arrived, the police found the chair Vera kicked away to hang herself mysteriously set upright against the wall. We learn that Isaac Morris, who hired Lombard and Blore and bought the island in the name of U. N. Owen, died of an apparent sleeping-pill overdose the night the guests arrived on the island. The police suspect that Morris was murdered. The police know that the people of Sticklehaven were instructed to ignore any distress signals from the island; they were told that everything taking place on the island was part of a game being played by the wealthy owners of the island and their guests.

The rest of the epilogue takes the form of a manuscript in a bottle, found by a fisherman and given to the police. It is written by Judge Wargrave, who writes that the manuscript offers the solution to an unsolved crime. He says he was a sadistic child with both a lust for killing and a strong sense of justice. Reading mysteries always satisfied him. He went into law, an appropriate career for him because it allowed him to indulge his zeal for death within the confines of the law. Watching guilty persons squirm become a new pleasure for him. After many years as a judge, he developed the desire to play executioner. He wanted to kill in an extraordinary, theatrical way, while adhering to his own sense of justice. One day, a doctor mentioned to Wargrave the number of murders that must go unpunished, citing a recently deceased woman he felt sure was killed by the married couple who worked as her servants. Because the couple withheld a needed drug in order to kill her, the murder could never be proven. This story inspired Wargrave to plan multiple murders of people who had killed but could not be prosecuted under the law. He thought of the "Ten Little Indian" rhyme that he loved as a child for its series of inevitable deaths.

Wargrave took his time gathering a list of victims, bringing up the topic of unpunished murders in casual conversations and hoping someone would mention a case of which they knew. Wargrave learned he was terminally ill and decided to kill himself after doing away with his victims. Wargrave's tenth victim, we learn, was Isaac Morris, who acted as his agent in making the arrangements for Indian Island, and who had been responsible for selling drugs to a young acquaintance of Wargrave, who subsequently killed herself. Before leaving for Indian Island, Wargrave gave Morris poison, which he claimed was a cure for Morris's indigestion.

Wargrave killed Marston and Mrs. Rogers first, he writes, because they bore the least responsibility for their crimes—Marston because he was born without a sense of moral responsibility, and Mrs. Rogers because she was under the sway of her husband when they murdered their elderly employer. Next he killed General Macarthur, sneaking up on him near the ocean. Wargrave goes on to describe how he tricked Armstrong into becoming his ally: Armstrong, he notes, "was a gullible sort of man . . . it was inconceivable to him that a man of my standing should actually be a murderer." He notes that he killed Mr. Rogers while the butler was out chopping sticks. At breakfast, he poisoned Emily Brent. Later, Armstrong agreed to help Wargrave fake his death, and pretended to examine the body of the judge and find a gunhot wound on his forehead. Wargrave arranged to sneak out and meet the Armstrong by the shore that evening. There, he pushed Armstrong over a cliff into the ocean.

After Armstrong's death, Wargrave returned to his room and played dead. Killing Blore was easy, since the ex-policeman foolishly came up to the house alone, and Wargrave then watched with satisfaction as Vera disposed of Lombard. Wargrave writes that he would have killed Vera himself, but he wanted to make her death fit the rhyme, so he set up her room in a suggestive way, with a noose hanging down and the smell of the sea wafting in, letting Vera's own guilt drive her to suicide.

Wargrave says he wrote the manuscript because he takes an artist's pleasure in his own work and wants recognition. He wonders if the police will pick up on three clues: first, that Wargrave was the odd man out—he was not really guilty of a murder, as the rest were, since in condemning Edward Seton to death he condemned a guilty man. Second, the line about the "red herring" points to the fact that Armstrong was somehow tricked into his death. Third, Wargrave's death by a bullet through the forehead will leave a red mark like the brand of Cain, the first murderer in the biblical book of Genesis.

Wargrave closes by describing the mechanism by which he will pull the trigger of the revolver from a distance and have the revolver flung away by an elastic band, thereby shooting himself so that he falls back on his bed as though laid there by the others. He concludes that men from the mainland "will find ten dead bodies and an unsolved problem on Indian Island."

ANALYSIS: EPILOGUE

The traditional detective story ends with a scene in which the sleuth, having carefully considered all the evidence, gathers the characters together and explains everything that has happened, concluding by unmasking the killer. Something similar takes place in the epilogue to *And Then There Were None*, although the police detectives are utterly baffled by what has transpired, and it is left to another character to explain things and untangle the mystery. Here, this other character is Wargrave, the murderer. Instead of being investigated and solved by a master detective, the ten murders in this novel can be solved only by the man who has committed them.

The unorthodox structure of this plot begins to make sense when we consider the themes that Christie has been exploring: specifically the effects of conscience and the administration of justice. These are classic detective-fiction themes, but Christie gives them a different spin by making her murder victims guilty of other murders unpunishable by any legal means. One can argue that the killings on Indian Island are not crimes at all but rather acts of ultimate justice. Wargrave is not killing for personal gain; rather, he is simply doing with his own hands what he did through the agency of law while he was still a judge. Seen in this light, Christie's decision to have him play the detective role and explain the mystery to the reader makes a certain kind of sense. In a traditional mystery story, the detective is the agent of justice, stepping in when a crime has been committed and assuring that the murderer is duly punished. In this story, Wargrave is doing exactly that, albeit by stepping outside the bounds of the law and becoming a killer himself.

Of course, there are objections to seeing Wargrave's actions as just. For example, one might point out that not all the crimes that he punishes are really deliberate and premeditated murders. However much we may despise Emily Brent, for instance, she did not actually kill her servant; Emily merely fired her, and the servant committed suicide. Similarly, however appalling a human specimen Tony Marston may be, his running over of two children was accidental. The same lack of malice characterizes Dr. Armstrong, who did not intend to kill the woman who died on his operating table. Armstrong and Marston's actions may have been heinous, but one could argue that they don't deserve to die. Christie goes out of her way to make us sympathize with Wargrave's victims, despicable though their actions may have been.

Wargrave himself, meanwhile, is a markedly unsympathetic character. He presents himself as an agent of justice, but he admits to experiencing a perverse pleasure in the taking of life, beginning with the "various garden pests" that he killed as a boy and continuing through his human victims. He is just but not at all merciful, and he kills with enthusiastic cruelty. He is also grandiosely arrogant; his conception of himself as an "artist" reduces his victims from human beings to mere means toward his selfish ends. Indeed, he writes his confession only because he cannot bear the idea that his perfect crime will go unappreciated.

At its conclusion, Christie's novel both does and does not reassert moral order. Wargrave's actions do not go unpunished; he shares the same fate as the people he has murdered. He has become a murderer himself, and so, under his own code of justice, he cannot be allowed to live. In this regard, Christie returns to the neat moral symmetry of the classic detective story: the guilty receive what they deserve, and no one gets away with murder. At the same time, however, Wargrave would have died of a terminal illness in any case, and by killing himself he merely asserts authority over death. He arranges his death in a way that thrills him, and dies a happy man and a proud artist. Christie allows us to feel the satisfaction of finally understanding the mystery, but she does not allow us the satisfaction of seeing the murderer sniveling, angrily led away in handcuffs, or humiliated in front of the world. Wargrave never loses his control or his murderous sense of justice.

Important Quotations Explained

1. There was a silence—a comfortable replete silence.
    Into that silence came The Voice. Without warning,
    inhuman, penetrating . . . "Ladies and gentlemen!
    Silence, please! . . . You are charged with the following
    indictments."

This quotation comes from the beginning of Chapter III, when the guests have just finished their first meal on Indian Island. Before this moment in the novel, Christie has established a general mood of foreboding and has hinted that all of her characters have guilty secrets. Now these secrets are brought into the open by the recorded voice. We begin to realize that these people have been brought to Indian Island for some sinister purpose having to do with their past crimes. The way the voice presents the list of crimes ("You are charged with the following indictments") serves as an important clue to the murderer's identity. The guests are charged with their murders in the formal style of a courtroom, in the language that Judge Wargrave was accustomed to using during his career.

2.   Mr. Owen could only come to the island in one way. It
     is perfectly clear. Mr. Owen is one of us.

These words from Wargrave in the middle of Chapter IX mark the
second crucial turning point in the novel (the first occurs when the
recorded voice accuses the guests of murder). Prior to this moment,
everyone has assumed, at least publicly, that their homicidal host,
Mr. Owen, is hiding somewhere on the island and planning to murder them. But after Lombard, Blore, and Armstrong conduct an
exhaustive search of the island and find no one, Wargrave boldly
states the only plausible conclusion: the killer is one of their party.
He speaks aloud what many of the others have considered but kept
to themselves. This realization fosters paranoia and suspicion that
build as the novel goes on and everyone begins to suspect someone
different. This quotation also marks the point at which Wargrave
steps in as leader of the group, a role he occupies until his apparent
death four chapters later.

3. Do they keep bees on this island? . . . It's sane enough what I'm asking. Bees, hives, bees! . . . Six little Indian boys playing with a hive.

Vera utters these sentiments early in Chapter XI, just after Mr. Rogers has been found dead in the woodshed. She becomes hysterical and points out that the murders have been patterned after the deaths in the "Ten Little Indians" poem that hangs in everyone's room. Rogers, the third person killed, was murdered with an ax while he was getting firewood, and the corresponding verse reads "Seven little Indian boys chopping up sticks; / One chopped himself in halves and then there were six." Vera's wild reference to "[b]ees, hives, bees" reflects her realization that the next murder will be carried out to correspond to the line "Six little Indian boys playing with a hive; / A bumblebee stung one and then there were five." She raves impatiently because the others do not understand, or do not want to admit, what is going on.

The poem is the novel's dominant motif, and it adds an air of supernatural inevitability to the murders. We know that just as each successive verse of the poem brings the death of another Indian boy, so will each character on the island be killed off in sequence.

4.   Dr. Armstrong . . . raised the wig. It fell to the floor,
      revealing the high bald forehead with, in the very
      middle, a round stained mark from which something
      had trickled . . . Dr. Armstrong . . . said—and his voice
      was expressionless, dead, far away: "He's been shot."

This passage comes from the end of Chapter XIII, when the group
of guests finds what appears to be the corpse of Judge Wargrave.
In fact, only Dr. Armstrong examines the body, and only he
declares that Wargrave has died from a shot to the head. We discover later that Armstrong has agreed to help Wargrave fake his
own death, going along with the ruse because he does not suspect
Wargrave of being the killer. The conspiracy gives Wargrave a free
hand, since no one but Armstrong knows that he is alive. As long
as no one sees him, Wargrave can do as he pleases and no one will
suspect him.

    There is little to help us deduce that Wargrave is not actually
dead. We share the perception of the remaining guests, who
assume that Wargrave has died and has thus been eliminated as a
suspect. By not telling us exactly what transpires, Christie breaks
the rules of the traditional detective story, in which the reader can,
theoretically, examine the clues and solve the mystery. This rule-
breaking dramatically increases the novel's suspense, since, with
Wargrave's faked death, subsequent events seem inexplicable and
almost supernatural.

5.   I have wanted . . . to commit a murder myself. I
recognized this as the desire of the artist to express
himself! . . . But—incongruous as it may seem to
some—I was restrained and hampered by my innate
sense of justice. The innocent must not suffer.

This quotation is taken from Judge Wargrave's written confession, which appears in the epilogue to the novel. In this passage, Wargrave explains how he hatched the idea of bringing a group of unpunished murderers to Indian Island and killing them off. Killing people who committed crimes unpunishable under the law satisfied both his desire to murder and his desire to mete out justice for wrongdoing.

This combination of murderous zeal and obsession with justice leaves Wargrave occupying a paradoxical place in the novel. He is both the murderer and the detective in this mystery, both the agent of death and the agent of justice. He is not a likable character, and our sympathies lie with the other people on the island, even with the ones clearly guilty of murder. But in a sense, Wargrave does act according to just principles, killing those, including himself, who are themselves responsible for the deaths of others.

QUOTATIONS

KEY FACTS

FULL TITLE
And Then There Were None (originally published as *Ten Little Indians)*

AUTHOR
Agatha Christie

TYPE OF WORK
Novel

GENRE
Murder mystery

LANGUAGE
English

TIME AND PLACE WRITTEN
1939, England

DATE OF FIRST PUBLICATION
1939

PUBLISHER
G. P. Putnam's Sons

NARRATOR
The narrator is an unnamed omniscient individual.

POINT OF VIEW
The point of view constantly shifts back and forth between each of the ten characters.

TONE
The narrator relates the story in a dark, foreboding, and sinister tone, and often reacts dramatically (or melodramatically) to the events of the story.

TENSE
Past

SETTING (TIME)
1930s

SETTING (PLACE)
Indian Island, a fictional island off the English coast

PROTAGONIST
Although no clear protagonist exists, Vera Claythorne and Philip Lombard are the most fully developed characters, and they outlive almost everyone else.

MAJOR CONFLICT
An anonymous killer gathers a collection of strangers on Indian Island to murder them as punishment for their past crimes.

RISING ACTION
The accusations made by the recorded voice turn the island getaway into a scene of paranoia; the murders of Tony Marston, Mrs. Rogers, General Macarthur, Mr. Rogers, and Emily Brent indicate that no one will be able to escape the "Ten Little Indians" rhyme.

CLIMAX
The apparent death of Judge Wargrave and the disappearance of Dr. Armstrong strip away any sense of order.

FALLING ACTION
The murders of Blore, Lombard, and Vera, combined with Wargrave's confession, restore some sense of order to the chaos of the story.

THEMES
The administration of justice; the effects of guilt on one's conscience; the danger of reliance on class distinctions

MOTIFS
The "Ten Little Indians" poem; dreams and hallucinations

SYMBOLS
The storm; the mark on Judge Wargrave's forehead; food

FORESHADOWING
Vera's first sight of Indian Island, which she thinks looks sinister, hints at the trouble to come; the old man's warning to Blore on the train that the day of judgment is approaching hints that Blore will soon die; the "Ten Little Indians" poem lays out the pattern for the imminent murders; Vera's fascination with both the poem and the hook on her ceiling presage her eventual decision to hang herself.

KEY FACTS

STUDY QUESTIONS & ESSAY TOPICS

STUDY QUESTIONS

1.   *Discuss the narrative techniques that Christie uses to create and maintain suspense throughout the novel.*

And Then There Were None uses a variety of techniques to create a foreboding, suspenseful mood. Foreshadowing adds tension, as when the old man on the train warns Blore of the approach of "judgment." The landscape of the island sometimes seems eerie and threatening, as does the weather: during much of the novel, Indian Island is cut off from the mainland by a severe storm whose violence and fury parallels the bloody events unfolding on the island. Psychological suspense also builds: even before the murders begin, the characters feel guilt and foreboding, and, as the novel progresses, they begin to suffer from nightmares, hysterical fits, and hallucinations that amplify the air of impending doom.

Christie also employs a constantly shifting point of view to build suspense. She gives us a glimpse of the action from one character's perspective and then races on to another point of view and then another. Each snippet is calculated to make the character in question seem suspicious. In Chapter II, for example, when the guests have just arrived on the island, Christie cuts abruptly from one character to the next as they prepare for dinner. Dr. Armstrong feels inspired by the beauty of the island to "make plans, fantastic plans"; Anthony Marston lies in his bath thinking to himself that he "must go through with it"; Blore ties his tie and hopes he will not "bungle" his "job"; Macarthur wishes he could "make an excuse and get away ... Throw up the whole business." Emily Brent reads Bible verses about the just punishment of sinners, and Lombard looks like a beast of prey. With this sequence of snippets, Christie gives us just enough access to each character's thoughts to make him or her seem like a potential murderer, and then shifts to the next character. She continues this technique throughout the novel, even as the number of suspects dwindles, so that we are never sure whom we should suspect most.

2. *Discuss the weaknesses of Dr. Armstrong, William Blore, Philip Lombard, and Vera Claythorne, and explain how Wargrave exploits these weaknesses as he carries out his plot.*

Aside from Wargrave, the last four characters left alive on the island are Armstrong, Blore, Lombard, and Vera. They are all on their guard, yet Wargrave is able to do away with all four of them by exploiting their weaknesses. Armstrong's weakness is his firm belief that class defines character. He cannot believe that a man of Wargrave's stature could be a murderer. Thus, he agrees to help Wargrave fake his own death, and willingly meets Wargrave out by the cliffs late at night, where it is a simple matter for Wargrave to push him over. Blore's weakness is his foolhardiness—he goes alone to the house to fetch food and so makes an easy target for Wargrave. Lombard, with his gun and his experience in dangerous situations, is a formidable foe, but his weakness is his refusal to believe that women are capable of violence. Vera is thus able to steal his gun and kill him with it. Vera's weakness is hysteria. She is susceptible to the power of suggestion and tormented by her guilt. Wargrave plays upon these weaknesses as he sets up a noose in Vera's room and thus compels the half-hypnotized Vera to hang herself.

3.   *What do you make of Christie's decision to violate the
      standard rules of mystery writing by making it nearly
      impossible for us to solve the mystery of* And Then There
      Were None *by ourselves? How does the unusual plot
      affect the experience of reading the novel?*

And Then There Were None can be criticized as an unfair mystery
novel. In a standard mystery story, a crime is committed, a detective
comes in to solve the crime, and the reader follows along with the
detective, learning everything the detective learns, and collecting
clues that would theoretically enable the reader to guess the identity
of the killer. At the close of such a mystery, the detective usually
gathers the remaining characters together, reveals the identity of the
murderer, and explains how the crime was committed.

   And Then There Were None breaks all of these rules. First, there
is no tidy arrest: the murderer gets away with his crime, and we discover his identity only because he leaves a confession behind. The
only outside detective is a policeman who arrives too late to accom-
plish anything and who is utterly baffled by what has happened.
Most unconventionally, the novel deceives us: we believe that Judge
Wargrave is dead, and so we no longer suspect him. In fact, he is still
alive, and he is the killer.

   In some ways, however, *And Then There Were None* is a very
conventional murder mystery. Ten people are isolated and cannot
escape; suspicion falls on all of the characters; red herrings abound;
a satisfyingly neat ending is produced in which the murderer's
actions and motivations are explained, and the pieces of the puzzle
fit together tightly. Although Judge Wargrave is the killer, he also
plays the role of the detective, unmasking the criminal—himself—at
the end of the novel and explaining how everything transpired.
Though Christie breaks some rules, she does so to make the story all
the more suspenseful.

Suggested Essay Topics

1. Discuss the role of the poem "Ten Little Indians" in *And Then There Were None*. Why does the murderer choose to follow the poem so closely? What effect does this have on the characters?

2. Discuss how Christie portrays social hierarchies. What commentary is she making on her society's class system?

3. Do you think that Wargrave acts justly? Why or why not?

4. Discuss the various alliances that form throughout the novel—particularly those between Blore, Armstrong, and Lombard; between Armstrong and Wargrave; and between Vera and Lombard. How do these alliances affect events? What makes them break down?

5. Discuss the order in which the characters die. Why do some live longer than others? Do you think this is this entirely by design? Does the murderer ever seem to lose control of the situation?

QUESTIONS & ESSAYS

REVIEW & RESOURCES

QUIZ

1. Which character is a reckless driver?

    A. Tony Marston
    B. Dr. Armstrong
    C. Philip Lombard
    D. Judge Wargrave

2. What is the title of the nursery rhyme that hangs in everyone's room?

    A. "Ten Little Indians"
    B. "Little Bo-Peep"
    C. "Little Jack Horner"
    D. "Hey Diddle Diddle"

3. Why does Vera come to the island?

    A. She is a tabloid journalist and wants to confirm rumors about the island's ownership
    B. She is pursuing Lombard
    C. She has been invited to spend her summer holiday with Constance Culmington
    D. She has been hired as a secretary by someone calling herself Una Nancy Owen

4. How does the killer accuse the guests of committing murders?

    A. By sending them letters
    B. By speaking to them on a hidden loudspeaker
    C. By listing their crimes on a record that is played after dinner
    D. The killer does not accuse them but just begins killing them off

5. By which false name does Blore identify himself early in the novel?

    A. Maltravers
    B. Davis
    C. Owen
    D. Smithers

6. Where did Lombard leave twenty-one men to die?

    A. A battlefield in France
    B. The South Pole
    C. The African bush
    D. The Sahara Desert

7. In what style is the house built?

    A. Victorian
    B. Gothic
    C. Modern
    D. Georgian

8. How does General Macarthur die?

    A. From a bee sting
    B. He is pushed off a cliff
    C. He is shot
    D. From a blow to the head

9. What objects disappear, one by one, as each murder is committed?

    A. The guests' suitcases
    B. Figurines of Indians
    C. Cans of tongue
    D. China plates with pictures of Indians on them

10. "U. N. Owen" is associated with what, according to the judge?

    A. The United Nations
    B. The coordinates of the island
    C. The word "uno"
    D. The word "unknown"

REVIEW & RESOURCES

11. When is Mr. Rogers killed?

     A.   While he is chopping wood
     B.   While he is making breakfast
     C.   While he is asleep
     D.   While he is exploring the attic

12. What was the name of the man Vera loved?

     A.   Arthur Richmond
     B.   Philip Lombard
     C.   Edward Seton
     D.   Hugo Hamilton

13. How did Dr. Armstrong happen to kill a patient while operating on her?

     A.   He wanted her money
     B.   He was drunk
     C.   He was inexperienced
     D.   He was in love with her, and she had married another man

14. Which guest carries a revolver?

     A.   Vera
     B.   Wargrave
     C.   Lombard
     D.   Armstrong

15. Which guest is prone to hysterics?

     A.   Tony Marston
     B.   Una Owen
     C.   Vera Claythorne
     D.   Mr. Rogers

16. When Armstrong, Blore, and Lombard join forces to identify the murderer, which character do they not suspect?

     A.   Mr. Owen
     B.   Mr. Rogers
     C.   Macarthur
     D.   Beatrice Taylor

17. From what does Emily Brent die?

    A. A lethal injection
    B. A bee sting
    C. Poison in her drink
    D. A blow to the head

18. Which guest pretends to be killed?

    A. Armstrong
    B. Blore
    C. Lombard
    D. Wargrave

19. Why don't boats come from the mainland to rescue the guests?

    A. The guests don't want to be rescued
    B. "Owen" ordered the town not to send boats
    C. The weather is bad
    D. Boats arrive only once a week

20. How is Blore killed?

    A. A marble bear is dropped on his head
    B. He doesn't die
    C. He is hanged
    D. His drink is poisoned

21. Which of the following is used to kill Lombard?

    A. An oar
    B. His own revolver
    C. A caterpillar
    D. A marble bear

22. Which of the guests die by the seashore?

    A. Vera and Emily Brent
    B. Lombard, Blore, and Vera
    C. Lombard, Armstrong, and Macarthur
    D. Armstrong and Macarthur

23. How does Vera die?

    A. She shoots herself
    B. She is poisoned
    C. She drowns trying to swim to a rock
    D. She hangs herself

24. Who is the last of the ten to die?

    A. Vera
    B. Lombard
    C. Wargrave
    D. Rogers

25. How do the police determine the culprit's identity?

    A. They use clues gleaned from Vera's diary
    B. The find the killer alive when they arrive on the island
    C. They never solve the case
    D. The killer places a confession in a bottle, which is thrown in the sea and found by a fisherman

ANSWER KEY:
1: A; 2: A; 3: D; 4: C; 5: B; 6: C; 7: C; 8: D; 9: B; 10: D; 11: A;
12: D; 13: B; 14: C; 15: C; 16: D; 17: A; 18: D; 19: B; 20: A;
21: B; 22: C; 23: D; 24: C; 25: D

SUGGESTIONS FOR FURTHER READING

BARGAINNIER, EARL F. *The Gentle Art of Murder: The Detective Fiction of Agatha Christie.* Bowling Green, Ohio: Bowling Green University Popular Press, 1980.

BARNARD, ROBERT. *A Talent to Deceive: An Appreciation of Agatha Christie.* New York: Dodd, Mead, 1980.

FITZGIBBON, RUSSELL H. *The Agatha Christie Companion.* Bowling Green, Ohio: Bowling Green State University Popular Press, 1980.

LIGHT, ALISON. *Forever England: Femininity, Literature, and Conservatism Between the Wars.* New York: Routledge, 1991.

ROWLAND, SUSAN. *From Agatha Christie to Ruth Rendell: British Women Writers in Detective and Crime Fiction.* New York: Palgrave, 2001.

WAGONER, MARY. *Agatha Christie.* Boston: Twayne Publishers, 1986.

REVIEW & RESOURCES

SPARKNOTES STUDY GUIDES: